What
Is
Love?

What Is Love?

GOD is Love
and he who does not love
does not know GOD

Marcella A. Spence

 authorHOUSE®

AuthorHouse™ LLC
1663 Liberty Drive
Bloomington, IN 47403
www.authorhouse.com
Phone: 1-800-839-8640

Published by AuthorHouse   02/21/2014

ISBN: 978-1-4918-1668-4 (sc)
ISBN: 978-1-4918-1667-7 (e)

Library of Congress Control Number: 2013916989

CONTENTS

Dedication.....ix
Preface.....x

It Is Written.....1
The Argument.....2
The Law.....4
The Law Translated.....6

Thus It Is Written.....13
The Commandments of Grace.....14
The Law of Love.....15
The Law of Love Translated.....18

The Way of Love.....26
The Way of Love Translated.....28

What Is God's Love?.....32
The Love of God.....34
The Love of God Translated.....38

The Ultimate Act of Love.....45
Love in Action.....47
Love in Action Translated.....49

Where Did Love Start?.....52
The Source of Love.....54
The Source of Love Translated.....56

Love Everlasting.....58
Love Everlasting Translated.....59

CONTENTS

Poems by Marcella A. Spence.....61
What is Love?.....62
Love.....64
God Loves You.....65
Prayer of Grace.....66

Benediction.....67
Epilogue 68

Glossary.....69

Acknowledgements Permissions References.....77

About the Author.....81

This book is dedicated to:

THORNS

Without this experience I would not know what it is to be rooted deeply in God's Love or grounded securely on His Love. I would not have come to know the breadth-*lack of restriction*, the length-*in great detail* or the height-*extreme* and true depth-*intensity* of God's Love. Without the Love of God there is absolutely nothing that you can overcome. With His Love comes all the things that you need to make you better, stronger and more at peace. That peace that has no understanding.

THE POWER OF GOD'S LOVE

God's Love has:
The power to save......our soul
The power to cleanse...........our sin
The power to forgive.......our persecutors
The power to heal...................our infirmities
The power to eradicate.................our iniquities
The power to consume................our hatred
The power to alleviate.................our pain
The power to comfort..............our grief
The power to transform.....our minds
The power to remove.......our strife
**Let love for your fellow believers continue
and be a fixed practice with you, [never let it fail].
Hebrews 13:1**

I pray that this book will show all who experience deep pain how to push through, totally relying on God to overcome their pain.

PREFACE

Let Love master your emotions.
You cannot love if God is not within you.
God is the Author of Love.
To all who are not born again,
What you call love is merely deep affection.
For to truly love requires God to live inside of you.
Love endures all things.
God is Love.
The battles we endure
cannot be conquered without God's Love.
When God's Love abides within
you will not experience hatred, anger, malice,
discontent, jealousy, etc.
Love is the greatest gift from God.
Nothing can be conquered without
God's Love.

But earnestly desire and zealously cultivate the greatest and best gifts and graces. And yet I will show you a more excellent way [one that is better by far and highest of them all—LOVE].
1 Corinthians 12:31

So then [God's gift] is not a question of human will or human effort, but of God's mercy. [It depends not on one's willingness nor on his strenuous exertion as in running a race, but on God having mercy on him.]
Romans 9:16

IT IS WRITTEN . . . .

Hear O Israel: the Lord our God is one Lord [the only Lord].

And you shall love the Lord your God with all your [mind and heart and with your entire being and with all your might.

And these words which I am commanding you this day shall be [first] in your [own] mind and hearts; [then]

You shall whet and sharpen them so as to make them penetrate, and teach and impress them diligently upon the [minds and] hearts of your children, and shall talk of them when you sit in your house and when you walk by the way, and when you lie down and when you rise up. Deuteronomy 6:4-7

You shall not take revenge or bear any grudge against the sons of your people, but you shall love your neighbor as yourself. I am the Lord. Leviticus 19:18

THE ARGUMENT . . . .

This is my argument: The Law, which began 430 years after the agreement [concerning the coming Messiah], does not and cannot void the agreement previously established (ratified) by God, so as to cancel the promise and make it void.

For if the legacy [of the promise depends on observing] the Law [as these false teachers would like you to believe], it no longer [depends] on the promise; however, God gave it to Abraham [as a free gift solely] by virtue of His promise.

What then was the purpose of the Law? It was added [later on, after the promise, to disclose and expose to men their guilt] because of sins and [to make men conscious of the sinfulness] of sin; and it was intended to be in effect until Jesus (the Descendant, the Heir) should come, to and concerning Whom the promise has been made. And it [the Law] was prepared and established and selected through the means of angels [and was given] by the hand of a go-between [Moses, an intermediary person between God and man]. Galatians 3:17-19

For Christ is the end of the Law [the limit at which it ceases to be, for the Law leads up to Jesus Who is the completion of its kinds, and in Jesus the purpose which it was designed to accomplish is achieved. That is, the goal of the Law is completed in Jesus] as the paths of righteousness (right relationship with God) for everyone who trusts in and adheres to and relies on Jesus.

For Moses writes that the man who [can] practice the righteousness (perfect conformity to God's will) which is based on the Law [with all its complex orders] shall live by it. Romans 10:4-5

And all who depend on the Law [who are seeking to be justified by obedience to the Law of rituals] are under a curse and doomed to disappointment and destruction, for it is written in the Scriptures, Cursed (doomed to eternal punishment) be everyone who does not continue to live and remain by all the doctrines and commands written in the Book of the Law and to practice them.

Now it is evident that no person is justified (declared righteous and brought into right standing with God) through the Law, for the Scripture says, The man in right standing with God [the just, the righteous] shall endure through and out of complete trust and he who through complete trust is declared righteous and in right standing with God shall have eternal life.

But the Law does not rest on complete trust [does not require confidence, has nothing to do with complete trust], for it itself says, He who does them [the things prescribed by the Law] shall endure by them [not by complete trust].

Christ purchased our freedom [liberating us from the curse of the Law [and its condemnation] by [Himself] becoming a curse for us for it is written [in the Scriptures], Cursed is everyone who hangs on a tree (is crucified); Galatians 3:10-13

THE LAW

THE TEN COMMANDMENTS

THE DIVINE ORDER
Exodus 20:3-17

You shall have no other gods before or besides me.

You shall not make yourself any graven image [to worship it] or likeness of anything that is in the heavens above, or that is in the water under the earth; You shall not bow down yourself to them or serve them; for I the Lord your God am a jealous God, visiting the iniquity of the father upon the children to the third and fourth generation of those who hate Me, But showing mercy and steadfast love to a thousand generations of those who love Me and keep My commandments.

You shall not repeat the name of the Lord your God in vain [that is, lightly or frivolously, in false affirmations or profanely]; for the Lord will not hold him guiltless who takes His name in vain.

[Earnestly] remember the Sabbath day, to keep it holy (withdraw from common employment and dedicated to God). Six days you shall labor and do all work, But the seventh day is a Sabbath to the Lord your God; in it you shall not do any work, you or your son, your daughter, your manservant, your domestic animals, or the sojourner within your gates. For six days the Lord made the heavens and the earth, the sea, and all that is in them and rested the seventh day. This is why the Lord blessed the Sabbath day and hallowed it [set it apart for His purposes].

Regard (treat with honor, due obedience, courtesy) your father and mother, that your days may be long in the land that your God gives you.

4

You shall not commit murder.

You shall not commit adultery.

You shall not steal.

You shall not witness falsely against your neighbor.

You shall not covet your neighbor's house, your neighbor's wife, or his manservant, or his maidservant, or his ox, or his donkey, or anything that is your neighbor's.

THE LAW TRANSLATED

The Ten Commandments is a single entity. Stated explicitly in the first four commandments is Israel's responsibility to love God and serve Him only. These four are the apodictic laws. These are the laws that cannot be broken. There are no exceptions when it comes to the obedience of the law. These four laws established the boundaries under which Israel's relationship with God would be translated. They were obligated to follow these laws. Then there are the casuistic laws—case by case laws which applied to specific situations. (example . . . Exodus 21)

From the very beginning God raised the Israelites to be a unique nation. Since they had lived in Egypt for such a long time they began to worship the gods of Egypt. The Egyptians worshiped many gods. This is called polytheism—*the worship of many gods.* God was about to re-establish that there is only one true God. This is called monotheism—*one belief in the existence of one deity.* God is a jealous God. (Exodus 20:5) The worship of other gods and bowing down before them amounted to spiritual adultery (Matthew 5:27-28; James 4:4), a sin punishable by death. (Leviticus 20:10; John 8:4-5) God's anger and indignation was so strong against idolatry that His wrath would be visited from generation to generation of those who hated Him.

The third commandment prohibits the misuse and abuse of the name of God. God's name is connected with His person, power and presence. His name deserves the highest honor and respect. His name defines who He is and what He did for Israel. When we disrespect the name of God it is an indication that we disregard God.

The fourth commandment was to remember the Sabbath day to keep it holy, to make time to worship the one true God. When God finished creating the earth, He set aside a day to rest. The Sabbath (seventh day), this is the holy day, one dedicated to rest. (Genesis 2:2-3) God blessed the Sabbath day. He set it apart as His own and hallowed it. God rested from all His work which He had created and done. We must magnify and worship God and give God the Glory that is due Him. A time also to come together in God's gracious love. All of God's people need rest and renewal of the journey we face tomorrow.

The fifth commandment entreats us to regard (treat with honor, due obedience, courtesy) your father and mother, that your days may be long in the land that the Lord your God gives you. One of the definitions of honor is consideration due or paid, as to worth, respectful regard.

At the age of 42 I was feeling a great sense of loss. Someone I've known for 26 years went home to be with the Lord. I only then realized how much of an impact she made on my life. At 48 also, I lost someone else who had the same impact on my life and the lives of my children. They were sisters and they filled the role of mother, father, teacher, friend and nurse—*which was their trained profession.* We don't always realize how much people can influence our lives until they are gone. Thank God that I had that insight and was able to tell them thank you before they passed. Their influence was so great that I had guilt feelings about how I felt about my parents. As I was thinking about it, that still small voice said, "Honor thy father and mother." Circumstances happens that puts distance between parent(s) and child(ren). Not everyone can fulfill the role(s) in life that they are given or sometimes thrust into. We are not perfect without God. Romans 3:22c-23 says,—For there is no distinction. Since all have sinned and are falling short of the honor and glory which God bestows and receives. I love my parents and have a great deal of respect for them and that is what God expects of us. You see, you can't respect if you do not love. If we say we love God then that means that God's Love is inside of us. We are required to love everyone with the love that's within. If we have respectful regard for our parents we are keeping God's Command. If you have to do so from afar, so be it. For sometimes close proximity only brings anger, hatred, frustration, confusion, etc. Still, it must be dealt with, otherwise you end up out of line with God's Law. Until a resolve is made expect the feelings, whatever they may be, to resurface continually. Last but not least, always, always pray for them. Pray that you can accept them as they are. Remember 1 Peter 2:17— Show respect for all men [treat them honorably]. Love the brotherhood (the Christian fraternity of which Christ is the Head). Reverence God. Honor the emperor-*government-those above you.*

Have you ever wondered why you should not murder? In the Bible, the soul is said to be in the blood because blood is so intimately involved in the life process. God's Word says: "For the life (the animal soul) is in the blood, and I have given it for you upon the altar to make atonement for your souls; for it is the blood that makes atonement by reason of the life [which it represents]. (Leviticus 17:11; Romans 3:24-26) For like reason, but making the connection even more direct, the Bible says: "The soul of every sort of flesh is in its blood." (Leviticus 17:14) Life is sacred. Therefore, blood in which the creature life resides is sacred and is not to be tampered with. Noah, the ancestor of all persons today living on the earth, was allowed by God to add flesh to his diet after the flood, but he was strictly commanded not to eat blood. At the same time he was commanded to show respect for the life, the blood, of his fellowman. **(Genesis 9:3-6)**

Taking Life

With God is the source of life. (Psalm 36:9) Man cannot give back a life when he takes it. "All the souls—to me they belong," says God. (Ezekiel 18:4) Therefore, to take a life is to take God's property. Every living thing has a purpose and a place in God's creations. No man has the right to take life except where God permits and in the way that He instructs. After the flood, God kindly allowed man to add flesh to his diet. God required that man acknowledge the life of the creatures as belonging to God by pouring the blood on the ground of any wild animal caught in hunting and covering the blood with dust. This was like giving it back to God and not using it for one's own purpose. (Leviticus 17:13) In the case of the animals brought to the sanctuary as communion offerings, in which the priest and the one bringing the sacrifice (and his family) has a share in the meal, the blood was drained out on the ground.

Man is entitled to enjoy the life that God has granted him and anyone who deprived him of that life will be answerable to God. This was demonstrated in what God said to Cain; "The voice of your brother's blood is crying out to me from the ground." (Genesis 4:10) Even one hating his brother and so wishing him dead or slandering him or bearing false witness against him, so as to endanger his life, would bring guilt onto himself in connection with the blood of his fellowman. (Matthew 19:18; Lev. 19:16; Deut 19:18-21; 1 John 3:15)

The value of life is considered so sacred by God that the blood of a murdered person is regarded by Him as contaminating the earth, and such contamination can only be cleansed by the shedding of the blood of the murderer. (Leviticus 24:17) On this basis the Bible authorizes capital punishment for murder, through duly constituted authority. (Numbers 35:33; Genesis 9:5-6)

One Proper Use Under Mosaic Law

There was only one proper use of blood, one legally proper under the Law. That was its use for sacrifice. Since life belongs to God, the blood was His and it was offered as a sin atonement (Leviticus 17:11) The pouring out of blood of animals used for food prevented misuse of blood, such as eating it or offering it to other gods. The man pouring the blood on the ground acknowledged God as the Giver of life and the need of sin atonement through the offering of a life.—(Leviticus 16:6, 11)

Under Christian Terms

In the Christian terms, the holiness of blood was strongly affirmed. No longer was animals to be offered, for those animal offerings were only a shadow of the reality, Jesus Christ. (Colossians 2:17; Hebrews 10:2-4, 8-10) The High Priest in Israel took a token portion of the blood into the Most Holy of the earthly Sanctuary. (Leviticus 16:14) Jesus Christ, as the real High Priest entered into heaven itself, not with His blood, which was poured out on the ground (John 19:34), but with the value of His perfect human life as represented by blood. This life right He never forfeited by sin, but retained it as useable for sin atonement. (Hebrews 7:26; 8:3; 9:11-12) For these reasons Christs' Blood cries out for better things than the blood of righteous Abel. Only the blood of the perfect sacrifice of the Son of God can call for mercy, while the blood of the martyred followers of Christ cries out for vengeance. (Hebrews 12:24; Revelations 6:9-11) These passages about Law #6 on "Thou shall not commit murder, were taken from and [2]*Used with permission from Aid to Bible Understanding (1971) published by Watchtower, Bible and Tract Society of Pennsylvania.*

What is adultery? Voluntary sexual intercourse between a married person and a partner other than the lawful spouse. In the Bible there are three types of people. The natural man, the spiritual man and the worldly man. The natural man does not know God. The spiritual man knows God and obeys His commands and the worldly man knows God but does not obey. He lives life in his own strength. He follows after other gods for satisfaction and fulfillment from the world and not God. He is committing spiritual adultery. God is a jealous God. God's anger and indignation toward idolatry is strong. 1 Corinthians 2:14-15

The eight commandment, Do not steal. Do not take what does not belong to you without asking. Some people make it a career to steal. Some steal out of necessity. Either way, it is against God's law. If that was you, and now you have been born again, Ephesians 4:28 admonishes, Let the thief steal no more, but rather let him be industrious, making an honest living with his own hands, so that he may be able to give to those in need.

A lie is a lie, is a lie. Thou shall not witness falsely against your neighbor. Why do you think God made a law about falsely accusing your neighbor? God knows and understands the function and capability of each part of our body and the organs of our body. So let's look at the tongue. The tongue is known as an organ of speech. *An instrument of communication.* It is said that the tongue is the strongest muscle in the body. The tongue is actually made up of a group of muscles that allow us to taste, swallow and talk. Let's look at what the Bible says about the tongue. James 3:6-10 . . . And the tongue is a fire. [The tongue is a] world of wickedness set among our members, contaminating and depraving the whole body and setting on fire the wheel of birth (the cycle of man's nature), being itself ignited by hell (Gehenna). But the human tongue can be tamed by no man. It is a restless (undisciplined— *not trained or developed by teaching or control,* irreconcilable—*cannot be brought to acceptance*) evil, full of deadly poison. With it we bless the Lord and Father, and with it <u>we curse men who are made in God's likeness!</u> There is a simple message here, when you get ready to curse someone out, to give them a piece of your mind, think twice, they, just like you are made in the image of God. So who are you really cursing?— Out of the same mouth come forth blessing and cursing. These things, my brethren, ought not to be so. Proverbs 25:18 says: A man who bears false witness against his neighbor is like a heavy sledge hammer and a sword and a sharp arrow. The blow from a sledge hammer can kill, a sword cuts and a sharp arrow pierces. Do you think Solomon got his point across? Let's go to Proverbs 6 and see the six things that God hates and the seventh an abomination. Verses 16-19—a proud look, a lying tongue, hands that shed innocent blood, a heart that manufactures wicked thoughts and plans, feet that are swift in running to evil, a false witness who speaks lies, [even under oath] and he who sows discord among his brethren. For it is written . . . Exodus 23:1-3, 6-8—You shall not repeat or raise false a report; you shall not join with the wicked to be an unrighteous witness.—You shall not follow a crowd to do evil; nor shall you bear witness at a trial so as to side with a multitude to pervert justice.—Neither shall you be partial to the poor man in his trial [just because he is poor].—You shall not pervert justice due to the poor in his cause.—Keep far from a false matter and [be very careful] not to condemn to death the innocent and the righteous, for I will not justify and acquit the wicked.—You shall take no bribe, for the bribe blinds those who have sight and perverts the testimony and the cause of the righteous. False witnessing was punishable by the same penalty as the accused would receive. Here are other references: Deut. 17:5-7; 19:15-21; Proverbs 19:9

The same way that a tongue can cause damage, it can also heal. Proverbs 25:15—By long forbearance and calmness of spirit a judge or ruler is persuaded, and soft speech breaks down the most bonelike resistance. Here are some examples of soft speech. My favorite: 1 Samuel 25:24: After Nabal insulted David's kindness and Abigail, Nabal's wife, learned of it, she made haste to preserve lives. Kneeling at David's feet she said, "Upon me alone let this guilt be my lord, and let your handmaid, I pray you, speak in your presence and hear the words of your hand maid" . . . . you know the rest of the story . . . . vs. 35. Proverbs 15:1-2—A soft answer turns away wrath; but grievous words stir up anger, the tongue of the wise utters knowledge rightly, but the mouth of the [self-confident] fool pours out folly. Then vs. 4, A gentle tongue [with its healing power] is a tree of life, but willful contrariness in it breaks down the spirit.

The tenth commandment in today's standard simply breaks down to this: You shall not covet—*to desire enviously that which belongs to another*— Your neighbor's home, your neighbor's wife, his butler or maid (or anyone in his employ), his ox—his work/occupation/work machines, his donkey—his mode(s) of transportation or anything that is your neighbor's.

As we, the body of Christ come together to worship Him, our faith is strengthened and we will become stronger as a community of believers. Prayer gives us the power to overcome the world. It is not merely hearing the Law [read] that makes one righteous before God, but it is the doers of the Law who will be held guiltless and acquitted and justified. Romans 2:13

The Law of God is not given to provide a series of maxims that will enable us to achieve some lofty spirituality.

THUS IT IS WRITTEN . . . .

The first man Adam became a living being (an individual personality); the last Adam (Christ) became a life-giving Spirit [restoring the dead to life].

But it is not the spiritual life which came first, but the physical and then the spiritual.

The first man [was] from out of the earth, made off dust (earthly-minded); the second Man [is] the Lord from out of heaven.

Now those who are made of the dust are like him who was first made of the dust (earthly-minded); and as is [the Man] from heaven, so also [are those who are of heaven (heavenly-minded).

And just as we have borne the image [of the man] of dust, so shall we and so let us also bear the image [of the man] of heaven. **1 Corinthians 15:45-49**

For the heart (the understanding, the soul) of this people has grown dull (stupid, hardened and calloused), and their ears are heavy and hard of hearing and they shut tight their eyes, so that they may not perceive and have knowledge and become acquainted with their eyes and hear with their ears and understand with their souls and turn [to Me and be converted], that I may heal them. **Acts 28:27**

THE COMMANDMENTS OF GRACE

THE DIVINE RULE (Government)

And you shall love the Lord your God out of and with your whole heart and out of and with all your soul (your life) and out of and with your mind (with your faculty of thought and moral understanding) and out of and with all your strength.

You shall love your neighbor as yourself. **Mark 12:30-31**

Make it a practice to love your enemies.

Invoke blessings upon your enemies.

Pray for your enemies.

Offer the other cheek when they strike you.

Give to him your undergarment when they take your outer garment.

Give to the poor and needy.

Do not demand back what was taken from you.

Treat others the way you want to be treated.

Lend expecting no return, give considering it no loss.

Be merciful. Because your Father is merciful. **Luke 6:27-36**

THE LAW OF LOVE

Mark 12:30-31
Luke 6:27-36

And you shall love the Lord your God out of and with your whole heart and out of and with your soul (your life) and out of and with all your mind (with your faculty of thought and your moral understanding) and out of and with all your strength. This is the first and principle commandment.

The second is like it and is this, You shall love your neighbor as yourself. There is no other commandment greater than these.

But I say unto you who are listening now to Me: [in order to heed, make it a practice to] love your enemies, treat well (do good to, act nobly toward) those who detest you and pursue you with hatred,

Invoke blessings upon and pray for the happiness of those who curse you, implore God's blessing (favor) upon those who abuse you [who revile, reproach, disparage, and high-handedly misuse you].

To the one who strikes you on the jaw or cheek, offer the other jaw or cheek also; and from him who takes away your outer garment, do not with hold your undergarment as well.

Give away to everyone who begs of you [who is in want of necessities], and of him who takes away from you your goods, do not demand or require them back again.

And as you would like and desire that men would do to you, do exactly so to them.

If you [merely] love those who love you, what quality of credit and thanks is that to you? For even the [very] sinners love their lovers (those who love them).

And if you are kind and good and do favors to and benefit those who are kind and good and do favors to and benefit you, what quality of credit and thanks is that to you? For even the preeminently sinful do the same.

And if you lend money at interest to those from whom you hope to receive, what quality of credit and thanks is that to you? Even notorious sinners lend money at interest to sinners, so as to recover as much again.

But love your enemies and be kind and do good [doing favors so that someone derives benefit from them] and lend, expecting and hoping for nothing in return but considering nothing as lost and despairing of no one; and then your recompense (your reward) will be great (rich, strong, intense, and abundant), and you will be sons of the Most High, for He is kind and charitable and good to the ungrateful and selfish and wicked.

So be merciful (sympathetic, tender, responsive, and compassionate) even as your Father is [all these].

Romans 2:11-13

For God shows no partiality [undue favor or unfairness; with Him one man is not different from another].

All who have sinned without the Law will also perish without [regard to] the Law, and all who have sinned under the Law will be judged and condemned by the Law.

For it is not merely hearing the Law [read] that makes one righteous before God, but it is the doers of the Law who will be held guiltless and acquitted and justified.

THE
COMMANDMENTS
OF
GRACE

THE
LAW
OF
LOVE

THE LAW OF LOVE
TRANSLATED

In John 14:15 Jesus said, "If you [really] love Me you will keep (obey) My commandments." To love is the greatest command in the Law of Love and the principle command of Christ.

There are four functions to the first command in the Law of Love or as they are also called the Commandments of Grace. **1.** You shall love God <u>out of and with</u> your whole heart means to love God from the inside to the outside—from the spiritual to the physical. As a child of God what is within you is spiritual and will reflect in your physical life. As a true Christian the Holy Spirit dwells within you. The day you said yes to Jesus you invited Him into your heart. You opened the door to a new life. (Revelations 3:20) So to love out of your whole heart is to love from your most essential and emotional center. The exhibition of your physical life is a reflection of what is inside of you; your lifestyle, your speech, your behavior. Your love or lack of love is always on display for the world to see. Can an unsaved person observe you and want what they see? Proverbs 4:23 says; to keep and guard your heart with all vigilance-*an alert watchfulness*-and above all that you guard, for out of it flows the springs-*source-one that supplies info* (Acts 3:15) into your life. So who is supplying information to your heart? For whatever is supplied into you will be what you give out. Now then, it goes on to say <u>with</u> your whole heart. With here means *⁵alongside-side by side.* Who and what is the source that is supplying your foundation? It should be God's Love. Once you know who's flowing out of your heart, they will also flow alongside with you. The choice is yours.

FFT-The soul of the heart is love.

2. Next is your soul. What is your soul? A soul is one's essence, which is the characteristics, traits, quality and attribute of a person that makes them what they are, their central nature, personality. We are not on this earth for ourselves. So to love God out of your soul is to love Him from

within with exactly who you are. Genesis 2:7 says, When the Lord breathed into you the breath of life He gave you your personality, your characteristics and made you into who you are. He gave you what you needed to become what He wanted you to be to do His work. God has assigned each of us a special calling, a purpose that benefits the kingdom of God. Pay no heed to what man thinks of you. God already knows who you are. After all, He made you.

FFT—*The heart of the soul is peace.*

3. Next . . . . and out of and with all your mind (with your faculty-*your inherent ability or power of the human mind,*-in thought-*ideas* and your moral understanding-*of right or wrong*). 1 Corinthians 2:15-16 gives insight to the spiritual man and his mind. As a result of God's Love, he—the spiritual man—tries all things [he examines, investigates, inquires into, questions and discerns all things], yet is himself to be put on trial and judged by no one [he can read the meaning of everything, but no one can properly discern or appraise or get an insight into him]. For who has known or understood the mind (counsels-*guidance* and purposes-*goals/aims*) of the Lord so as to guide and instruct Him and give Him knowledge? But we have the mind of Christ (the Messiah) and do hold the thoughts (feelings-*compassions* and purposes) of His heart. So what is in our mind should be that of Christ and it will manifest in our lifestyle.

FFT-*The soul of the mind is wisdom.*

4. Finally . . . . and out of and with your strength. What is your strength? It is your power, your authority, your firmness-*unwavering.* We are able to love God out of the same power that we receive from Him. John 1:12—But as many as did receive and welcome Him, He gave the power-*authority* to become the sons of God-Acts 1:8 . . . . the power to witness. We know God and the power of the resurrection-Philippians 3:10. God is my strength and power and makes my way perfect. 2 Samuel 22:33 (NKJV) Psalms 73:26 says, My flesh and heart may fail, but God is the Rock and firm strength of my heart and my [5]Portion-*a part, esp. that allotted to a person*—forever.

If you keep this command you are on your way to a victorious life because God will be your source—*the one that supplies* you within so that your manifestations will be that of a disciple. You will love Him out of and with-*which is side by side* your source. You will always be in-sync with Him. With these in place this command should be easy to do.

FFT—The soul of the strength is power.

Once you have love for yourself you will be able you to love your neighbor. Your neighbor is not just the person living next door to you. Your neighbor is sitting next to you right now. Your family member, those whom you work with and the stranger you pass on the street. The people you see at the bus stop and so on. First you need God's Love within you. If God's Love is not within you, you cannot, I repeat, you cannot share or exhibit love. God's Love within you makes you capable to first love yourself, then your neighbor and now your enemy. Once we get past the self-condemnations and the hang-ups we inflict on ourselves, whether it is our weight, our looks or whatever they are, we can love someone else. If you are ready for the truth and nothing but the truth, ask God to show you yourself as He sees you. Please be sure that you are ready to accept the truth of what God shows you. God's truth not people truth. Ask Him and He will help you to fix yourself, if necessary, then you can move on to loving others.

We all know that to love your enemy is not easy to do. It is very difficult to love your enemy but the command says to make it a <u>practice</u> to love your enemy. This means it will not happen overnight. Just like you have to practice when learning to do anything, you must practice loving your enemy. How do you do this? By first, forgiving them and then extending the white flag of surrender or the olive branch of peace. The next time you see them you can smile and say hello or just smile in passing. You can do that for a while and then next time say hello and say how are you today? If they do not respond to you don't let it bother you. Keep smiling and saying hello one day they might answer. Keep yourself open to do something nice like holding the door open and letting them go first if the opportunity permits. Keep practicing, not be harassing. There is actually Bible reference on this in Exodus 23:4-5. The rest of this command says to treat them well and do good and act nobly toward them and those who detest you and pursue you with hatred. Next, invoke blessing upon them. A simple 'God Bless you' and there are many examples in the Bible, here are a few: Numbers 6:24-26; Ruth 2:4; 1 Peter 5:14b; 2 Timothy 4:22.

Now in your blessing them be very careful that your heart is right. It must be done in love and sincerity or you will incur cursing upon yourself. Pray for their happiness. Pray sincerely for them for God to bless them. I promise that it is not easy at first but genuineness will come. In the beginning I suggest that you write the prayer for your enemy if you can't find the words to come. For some it is difficult in the beginning to pray for someone who did you wrong and caused you much pain.

When the pain is extremely great and you find it very difficult to forgive them, ask God to forgive them every time you pray. Also ask God to help you to forgive them. Soon you'll see that you can and will forgive them. There is pain that makes it hard to forgive. Jesus experienced that pain. He came to His own and His own received Him not and they scourged and crucified Him. Jesus' pain was so great He asked His Father to forgive them. We too can say "Father forgive them for they know not what they do." If you ask or wondering how can we too say that? As a result of what has happened, it has caused you to seek God and His strength which in time puts you on a higher and better communicable level with God. You've come to rely on God as your only source of strength. Jesus reached the highest level of honor because He loved, trusted, believed, clung and relied on God His Father to see him through. God knows exactly how you are feeling and He will see you through your pain. Don't try to go around it. Once you've truly forgiven, be aware, Satan will bring up guilt feelings. Immediately confess (out loud) that all has already been forgiven and move on.

I experienced a situation and due to this situation I was under advisory. Due to the unfairness of my situation my advisors became anxious to see me make my enemy my footstool Unknowingly I did not comply. If you turn to Acts 2:34-36, it says, For David did not ascend into the heavens, yet he himself says, The Lord (God) said to my Lord (Jesus), Sit at My (God) right hand and share My (God) throne until I make Your (Jesus') enemies a footstool for Your (Jesus') feet. Therefore let the whole house of Israel (whole earth) recognize beyond all doubt and acknowledge assuredly that God has made Him (Jesus) both Lord and Christ (the Messiah)—this Jesus whom you crucified. It is not for us to make our enemies our footstool. That is for God Himself to do in the manner He sees fit to do. Our command is to love our enemies with specific instruction on how to do so. It is not something that we would know how to do ourselves. For us to believe we are to make our enemies our footstool is what God wants us to do is false thinking. This would be a contradiction on God's part. The verse above represents what God the Father said to Jesus. When the time comes (and it is not here yet) God will make Jesus' enemies His footstool. Romans 12:19 says, Beloved <u>never</u> avenge yourselves, but leave the way open for [God's] wrath; for it is written, Vengeance is Mine, I will repay (requite), says the Lord. (Deuteronomy 32:35)

To the one who strikes you on the jaw or cheek, offer the other. This does not refer to a physical blow. This is the verbal attacks that you encounter. The slandering of your character, the insults, disrespectful comments said to you, about your family or your ministry. The attacks on your integrity. Hurtful acts done to make you ashamed or to bring shame to your family or ministry. The many false accusations made about you. The issues of your past that are brought up to cause embarrassment. We live in a world of technology where events and words can be manipulated to give a false impression. Many has the ability to orchestrate a truth. Because you see it or hear it does not always make it true. When this happens memorize these two scripture verses: Isaiah 54:4, 17. Speak them but most importantly believe them. Find as many scripture that deals with your situation and speak and believe them. Remember as a child of God you already have the victory.

And he who takes away your outer garment do not withhold your undergarment. This is the person who takes you to court and files a lawsuit against you. Give him what he is due and do not withhold from him if he has been wronged. Isaiah 59:4 says: None sues or calls in righteousness [but for the sake of doing injury to others—to take some undue advantage]; no one goes to law honestly and pleads [his case] in truth; they trust in emptiness, worthlessness and futility, and speaking lies! They conceive mischief and bring forth evil! We are not to sue our fellow Christians in Christ. Read 1 Corinthians 6:1-11 which is the Human Law. It is the human way of doing things.

Give to everyone who begs of you. This needs no explanation. To him who is in want of necessities. I would set aside a specific amount of money in my pocket or purse in case someone begged or asked me for money or purchase a hot meal for them. You let the Holy Spirit lead as the situation permits.

When someone steals from you (and especially if you know who did) do not demand it back. Instead (if possible) give them the exact same thing they stole from you. In love of course. This is not mandatory but it might help them to see that all they had to do was ask.

This one is easy, treat people the same way you want to be treated. When I became a mother a thought of mine was how were people going to treat my children. So I made it a personal priority to be polite, kind, respectful, considerate and compassionate to anyone I came in contact with. I figured if God considered David's offspring He would consider mine too. Don't forget to be patient, especially with the elderly.

If you [merely] love those who love you, what quality of credit-*essential attribute*-is that to you? For even the very sinners love their lovers (those who love them). This is self-explanatory. If you are kind and good and do favors to and benefit those who are kind and good and do favors to and benefit you, what quality of credit and thanks is that to you? For even the preeminently do the same. This is why God wants you to love your enemies and those who despise you. Love is like a muscle, it must be exercised. When you love those that love you, you are not using it. When you practice loving your enemies it disciplines your love performance. Soon your love over shadows all wrong, hate, malice, etc. 1 Peter 4:8 says, Above all things have intense and unfailing love for one another, for love covers a multitude of sins [forgives and disregards the offenses of others]. See also Proverbs 10:12. Eventually your love walk becomes a way of life and believe me it feels great. Oh, you don't need money to develop your love walk. Love cannot be bought. Ask God to show you ways to express love. Remember, this is for <u>His</u> glory.

And if you lend money at interest to those from whom you hope to receive, what quality of credit and thanks is that to you. Even notorious sinners lend money at interests to sinners, so as to recover as much again. But love your enemies and be kind and good [doing favors so that someone derives benefit from them] and lend expecting and hoping for nothing in return but considering nothing as lost and despairing of no one; and then your recompense (your reward) will be great (rich, strong, intense and abundant), and you will be sons of the Most High, for He is kind and charitable and good to the ungrateful and the selfish and wicked.

So be merciful (sympathetic, tender, responsive and compassionate) even as your Father is all these.

Romans 2: 11-13

For God shows no partiality [undue favor or unfairness, with Him one man is not different from another]. All who have sinned without the Law will also perish without [regard] to the Law—Before the Law was given to Moses man had no regard for sin, it was not recognized. Romans 5:13, sin was not charged to man's account. They lived the way they wanted to. Some followed the God of Abraham and the others worshiped their idols and gods.—And all who sinned under the Law will be judged and condemned by the Law.—For Christ is the end of the Law, the limits at which it ceases to be, for the Law leads up to Him who is the accomplishment of its kind, and in Him the purpose-*goal* which it was planned to accomplish is achieved. In Matthew 5:17, Jesus says, Do you think that I have come to do away with or undo the Law or the Prophets; I have come not to do away with or undo but to complete and achieve them.—That is, the purpose of the Law is accomplished in Him as the means-*way* of righteousness for everyone who trusts in and adheres to-*obeys* and relies on Him. (Romans 10:4)

For it is not merely hearing the Law [read] that makes one righteous before God,—Since we are justified through faith, let us [grasp the fact that we] have [the peace of reconciliation to hold and to enjoy] peace with God through our Lord Jesus Christ. Through Him we have [our] access by faith into the grace in which we [firmly and safely] stand. And let us rejoice and exult in our hope of experiencing and enjoying the glory of God. (Roman 5:1-2)—but it is the doers of the Law who will be held guiltless and acquitted and justified. And those whom He thus foreordained, He also called; and those whom He called, He also justified (acquitted, made righteous, putting them in right standing with

Himself). And those whom He justified, He also glorified [raising them to a heavenly worthiness and status or state of being]. (Romans 8:30) Christ practiced the righteousness (perfect conformity to God's will) which is based on the Law with all its intricate demands so now Jesus Lives. (Romans 10:5, Leviticus 18:5)

FFT—FOOD FOR THOUGHT

**The soul of the heart is LOVE
The heart of the soul is PEACE
The soul of the mind is WISDOM
The soul of the strength is POWER**

THE WAY OF LOVE

1 Corinthians 13

If I [can] speak in the tongues of men and [even] angels, but have not love (that reasoning, intentional, spiritual, devotion such as is inspired by God's love for and in us), I am only a noisy gong or a clanging cymbal.

And if I have prophetic powers (the gift of interpreting the divine will and purpose), and understand all the secret truths and mysteries and possess all knowledge, and if I have [sufficient] faith so that I can remove mountains, but have not love (God's love in me) I am nothing (a useless nobody).

Even if I dole out all that I have [to the poor in providing] food, and if I surrender my body to be burned or in order that I may glory, but have not love (God's love in me), I gain nothing.

Love endures long and is patient and kind; love never is envious nor boils over with jealousy, is not boastful or vainglorious, does not display itself haughtily.

It is not conceited (arrogant and inflated with pride); it is not rude (unmannerly) and does not act unbecomingly. Love (God's love in us) does not insist on its own rights or its own way for it is not self-seeking; it is not touchy or fretful or resentful; it takes no account of the evil done to it [it pays no attention to a suffered wrong].

It does not rejoice at injustice and unrighteousness, but rejoices when right and truth prevail.

Love bears up under anything and everything that comes, is ever ready to believe the best of every person, its hopes are fadeless under all circumstances, and it endures everything [without weakening].

Love never fails [never fades out or becomes obsolete or comes to an end]. As for prophecy (the gift of interpreting the divine will and purpose), it will be fulfilled and pass away; as for tongues, they will be destroyed and cease; as for knowledge, it will pass away [it will lose its value and be superseded by Truth].

For our knowledge is fragmentary (incomplete and imperfect), and our prophecy (our teaching) is fragmentary (incomplete and imperfect).

But when the complete and perfect (total) comes, the incomplete and imperfect will vanish away (become antiquated, void and superseded).

When I was a child, I talked like a child, I thought like a child, I reasoned like a child; now that I have become a man, I am done with childish ways and have put them aside.

For now we are looking in a mirror that gives only a dim (blurred) reflection [of reality as in a riddle or enigma], but then [when perfection comes] we shall see in reality and face to face! Now I know in part (imperfectly), but then I shall know and understand fully and clearly, even in the same manner as I have been fully and clearly known and understood [by God].

And so faith, hope, love abide [faith—conviction and belief respecting man's relation to God and divine things; hope—joyful and confident expectation of eternal salvation; love—true affection for God and man, growing out of God's love for and in us], these three; but the greatest of these is love.

THE WAY OF LOVE
TRANSLATED

Many call this the love chapter. It is read at many weddings. It becomes the subject of sermons in many pulpits in the month of February for Valentine's Day. This chapter, however, gives a descriptive as to the character of Love. That is, God's Love in us. Not our description of love. Without God's love in us all we have is a deep affection for one another. Affection is a fond or tender feeling towards another. So when you say "I love you," how can you give what you do not possess if you are not a child of God. If God's love is not in you, you cannot share or feel love. Let us now look at the characteristics of God's Love.

If you [can] speak in the tongues of men and [even] of angels,—If you speak many languages and even the language of angels but have not God's Love in you—that love which inspires an analyzing, purposely sacred worship with God, we are only making noise. It is like a thirst that needs to be satisfied. When you are thirsty it is a specific thirst and until you satisfy that specific thirst it is not quenched. An unquenched thirst eventually becomes a craving, then an addition; and we know how some addictions can spiral out of control. In God's Love we have this desire to seek Him daily . . . . you will seek (inquire for and require as necessity) the Lord your God, you will find Him if you [truly] seek Him with all your heart [and mind] and soul and life. (Deuteronomy 4:29)

And if we have prophetic powers (the gift of interpreting the divine will and purpose), understands all the secret truths and mysteries and possess all knowledge and even enough faith that we can move mountains, but have not God's love in us we are a useless nobody. Why? Because God's Love is power.

We can feed all the hungry and give all we have to the poor and needy, give our bodies to be burned so that we may gain status and glory but if we don't have God's Love in us we gain nothing.

God's Love bears up under suffering, enduring affliction or pain without anger or complaint and is warm hearted and friendly. It has no discontentment to boil over into jealously. It does not jubilant itself or will not make itself extravagantly showy and it does not have excessive self esteem and self importance.

Love is not arrogant and inflated with pride; it is not unmannerly and does not act ugly. Love (God's Love in us) does not insists on its own rights or its own way;—this means what it feels it is entitled to, what it wants to do—for it is not oversensitive, easily offended or anxious, irritable or objective. It takes no account of the evil done to it [it pays no attention to a suffered wrong]. It does not keep a ledger or journal of all the wrong it has experienced.

Love does not rejoice at unfairness and wrong doing against God's will, but rejoices when right and truth prevails.

Love bears up under anything and everything that comes its way. It is ever ready to believe the best of every person. Its hope does not weaken under all circumstances, and it endures everything [without weakening].

Love never fails,—this means that it never disappoints or is unsuccessful, it never fades out or becomes inexistent or comes to an end. As for prophecy (the gift for interpreting the divine will and purpose), it will be fulfilled and pass away; as for the languages,—A little note about languages: they were created by God and Jesus (Gen. 11:1-9, key verse 7) and on that glorious day we will have no need for languages any more.—they will be destroyed and cease, as for knowledge; it will pass away, it will lose its value and be superseded by Truth. What Truth? That Jesus Christ is the complete and perfect, the true Reality. (vs. 10 and 12)

Marcella A. Spence

For our knowledge is incomplete and imperfect and our teachings are incomplete and imperfect.

But when the complete and perfect—Jesus Christ—comes, the incomplete and imperfect will vanish away. The incomplete and imperfect will become out of date, void and be replaced.

When I was a child, I talked, thought and reasoned like a child—as a new Christian, a born again child of God, you have to be fed milk, you are spiritually immature . . . so be done with every trace of wickedness, [4]depravity-*corrupt*—malignity-*exhibiting ill will or spite,*—(these things tend to grow)—and all pretense and hypocrisy, grudges, slander and evil speaking of every kind. Like new born babies crave (thirst for, desire) milk, so you should crave the pure unpolluted spiritual milk, that by it you may be nurtured and grow into complete salvation, since you've already tasted the goodness and kindness of the Lord. (1 Peter 2:1-3) Matt 5:6 says, Blessed and fortunate and happy and spiritually prosperous (in that state in which the born again child of God enjoys this favor and salvation) are those who hunger and thirst after righteousness (uprightness and right standing with God), for they shall be <u>completely satisfied</u>!—Now that I have become a man, I am done with childish ways and have put them aside.—Hebrews 5:12-14 says, For even though by this time you ought to be teaching others, you actually need someone to teach you again the very first principles of God's Word. You have come to need milk (again) not solid food. For everyone who continues to feed on milk is obviously inexperienced and unskilled in the doctrine of righteousness (of conformity to the divine will in [4]purpose-*goal/aim*, [4]thought-*belief,* and action-*obedience*), for he is a mere infant [not able to talk yet]! But solid food is for full grown men (mature Christians) for those whose senses and mental [4]faculties-*abilities* are trained by practice to [4]discriminate-*differentiate* and distinguish between what is morally good and noble and what is evil and contrary either to divine or human law.

For now we are looking in a mirror that gives only a blurred reflection [of reality as in a mental puzzle or one that battles the understanding. We are now battling to gain understanding of this reality. But then when perfection comes—Jesus Christ—*the **Perfect** and **only** **example of***

30

Excellence, we shall see in reality-*truth* and face to face with perfection! Now we know imperfectly but then we shall know and understand fully and clearly, even in the same manner as I have been fully and clearly known and understood by God.

And so faith, hope, love lives [faith—*conviction and belief respecting man's relation to God and divine things*; hope—*joyful and confident expectation of eternal salvation*; love—*true affection for God and man*, ***growing out of God's Love for and in us***], these three; but the greatest of these is LOVE.

WHAT IS GOD'S LOVE?

The New Condensed Bible Dictionary and Concordance by Charles F. Pfieffer says: **Love is the single attribute of God**. All the things He has done, is doing and will do for you is because He loves you. **Love is the immediately noticeable moral excellence in the Christian's life**. Take note of the word "in", it's not "of", "for", or "to" a Christian's life. This love is the true affection for God and man. **Love is learned from God**. 1 John 4:19—We love Him because He first loved us. **Love is a test of discipleship**. John 13:35—By this all men will know that you are my disciples, if you love one another, [if you keep showing love among yourselves. **Obedience is a test of love**. John 13:14; 15:15—If you love me keep my commandments. **Love is the greatest command of the Laws and the primary command of Christ**. It is the first command in the Law of Love (Mark 12:30-31). Songs of Solomon 8:7 says, Many waters cannot quench love, neither can floods drown it. If a man would offer all the goods of his house for love, he would be utterly scorned and despised! Jesus was utterly scorned and despised. Because He loves you and me, Jesus gave Himself. He sacrificed Himself because of Love. God gave up His power and deity so that man can have eternal life in heaven.

God's Love [4]begets-*to father* joy, peace longsuffering, gentleness, goodness, faith, meekness and self-control. We know these to be the fruit of the Spirit. (John 4:24) This love in turn [4]breeds-*reproduces* Christian fellowship, witnessing, a Christian lifestyle—one pleasing to God, giving-*helping others, tithing, giving out of love for the furthering of the gospel,*—sharing and encouragement-*to the grieving and faint of heart.*

For God so greatly loved and dearly prized the world that He [even] gave up His only begotten (unique) Son, so that whoever believes in (trusts in, clings to, relies on) Him shall not perish (come to destruction, be lost) but have eternal (everlasting) life.

The Father loves the Son and has given (entrusted, committed) everything into His hand. John 3:16, 35

The Father dearly loves the Son and discloses to (shows) Him everything that He Himself does. And He will disclose to Him (let Him see) greater things yet than these, so that you may marvel and be full of wonder and astonishment.

So that all men may give honor (reverence, homage) to the Son just as they give honor to the Father, Who has sent Him.
John 5:20, 23

Jesus said to them, If God were your Father, you would love Me and respect Me and welcome Me gladly, for I proceeded (came forth) from God [out of His very presence]. I did not even come on My own authority or of My own accord (as self-appointed); but He sent Me.
John 8:42

THE LOVE OF GOD

John 15

I AM the True Vine, and My Father is the Vinedresser.

Any branch in Me that does not bear fruit [that stops bearing] He cuts away (trims off, takes away); and He cleanses and repeatedly prunes every branch that continues to bear fruit, to make it bear more richer and more excellent fruit.

You are cleansed and pruned already, because of the word which I have given you [the teachings I have discussed with you].

Dwell in Me, and I will dwell in you. [Live in Me, and I will live in you.] Just as no branch can bear fruit of itself without abiding in (being vitally united to) the vine, neither can you bear fruit unless you abide in Me.

I am the Vine; you are the branches, Whoever lives in Me and I in him bears much (abundant) fruit. However, apart from Me [cut off from vital union with Me] you can do nothing.

If a person does not dwell in Me, He is thrown out like a [broken-off] branch, and withers; such branches are gathered up and thrown into the fire, and they are burned.

If you live in Me [abide vitally united to Me] and My words remain in you and continue to live in your hearts, ask whatever you will, and it shall be done for you.

When you bear (produce) much fruit, My Father is honored and glorified, and you show and prove yourselves to be true followers of Mine.

I have loved you, [just] as the Father has loved Me; abide in My love [continue in His love with Me].

If you keep My commandments [if you continue to obey My instructions], you will abide in My love and live on in it, just as I have obeyed My Father's commandments and live on in His love.

I have told you these things, that My joy and delight may be in you, and that your joy and gladness may be of full measure and complete and overflowing.

This is My commandment: that you love one another [just] as I have loved you.

No one has greater love [no one has shown stronger affection] than to lay down (give up) his own life for his friends.

You are My friends if you keep on doing the things which I command you to do.

I do not call you servants (slaves) any longer, for the servant does not know what the master is doing (working out). But I have called you My friends, because I have made known to you everything that I have heard from My Father. [I have revealed to you everything that I have learned from Him.]

You have not chosen Me, but I have chosen you and I have appointed you [I have planted you], that you might go and bear fruit and keep on bearing, and that your fruit may be lasting [that it may remain, abide], so that whatever you ask the Father in My name [as presenting all that I AM], He may give it to you.

This is what I command you: that you love one another.

If the world hates you, know that it hated Me before it hated you.

If you belonged to the world, the world would treat you with affection and would love you as its own. But because you are not of the world [no longer one of it], but I have chosen (selected) you out of the world, the world hates and (detests) you.

Remember that I told you, A servant is not greater than his master [is not superior to him]. If they persecuted Me, they will also persecute you; if they kept My word and obeyed My teachings, they will also keep and obey yours.

But they will do all this to you [inflict all this suffering on you] because of [your bearing] My name and on My account, for they do not know or understand the One Who sent Me.

If I had not come and spoken to them, they would not be guilty of sin [would be blameless]; but now they have no excuse for their sin.

Whoever hates Me also hates My Father.

If I had not done (accomplished) among them the works which no one else ever did, they would not be guilty of sin. But [the fact is] now they have both seen [these works] and have hated both Me and My Father.

But [this is so] that the word written in their Law might be fulfilled, They hated Me without a cause.

But when the Comforter (Counselor, Helper, Advocate, Intercessor, Strengthener, Standby) comes Whom I will send to you from the Father, the Spirit of Truth Who comes (proceeds) from the Father, He [Himself] will testify regarding Me.

But you also will testify and be My witnesses, because you have been with Me from the beginning.

John 16:12-15; 22-24; 27-28; 33; 30-31

I have still many things to say to you, but you are not able to bear them or to take them upon you or to grasp them now.

But when He, the Spirit of Truth (the Truth-giving Spirit) come, He will guide you into all the Truth (the whole, full Truth). For He will not speak His own message [on His own authority]; but He will tell whatever He hears [from the Father; He will give the message that has been given to Him], and He will announce and declare to you the things that are to come [that will happen in the future].

He will honor and glorify Me, because He will take of (receive, draw upon) what is Mine and will reveal (declare, disclose, transmit) it to you.

Everything that the Father has is Mine. That is what I meant when I said that He [the Spirit] will take the things that are Mine and will reveal (declare, disclose, transmit) it to you.

So for the present you are also in sorrow (in distress and depressed), but I will see you again and [then] your hearts will rejoice, and no one can take from you your joy (gladness, delight).

And when that time comes, you will ask nothing of Me [you will need to ask Me no questions]. I assure you, most solemnly I tell you, that My Father will grant you whatever you ask in My Name [as presenting all that I AM].

Up to this time you have not asked a [single] thing in My Name [as presenting all that I AM]; but now ask and keep on asking and you will receive, so that your joy (gladness, delight) may be full and complete.

For the Father Himself [tenderly] loves you because you have loved Me and have believed that I came out from the Father. I came out from the Father and have come into the world; again, I am leaving the world and going to the Father.

I have told you these things, so that in Me you may have [perfect] peace and confidence. In the world you have tribulation and trials and distress and frustrations; but be of good cheer [take courage; be confident, certain, undaunted]! For I have overcome the world. [I have deprived it of power to harm you and have conquered it for you.]

Now we know that You are acquainted with everything and have no need to be asked questions. Because of this we believe that you [really] came from God.

Jesus answered them, Do you now believe? [Do you believe it at last?]

THE LOVE OF GOD
TRANSLATED

I am Jesus the Son, God is My Father.

Any believer in Me (Jesus) that does not endure the consequence (that stops enduring) My Father cuts away; and He purifies and constantly trims every Believer that continues to endure the consequence, to have a richer and a more excellent result,—notice He purifies and constantly trims and conditions. The more you continue to endure the consequence, it keeps you in line with God and His Word and God's plan for you. Without them we begin or tend to rely on our own self and abilities. Our tests and trials come so that we will keep our eyes on God. To keep our communication (prayer life and the reading of His Word) open with Him. To keep our fellowship intact with Him. Why must we go through? So that we can endure more, and have a richer and more excellent result. What is the excellent result? Your growth. It is like a rose plant, you prune and you clip it, you fertilize it in the late fall so that next year it will produce many more beautiful roses. Before a fruit tree produces fruit there is a blossom. The blossom goes through a process, with the help of bees, before the fruit appears. So it is with your spiritual growth. God constantly prunes and clips us so that our result will be an abundant life here and eternal life in heaven.

You are purified and trimmed already, because of the Word which He has already given you, the teachings that you received. The word which you heard before you accepted Christ into your heart and life. You are made pure and trimmed already upon acceptance of Christ the Lord of your life. Your life immediately changes inwardly. Once you've told your friend/family of your acceptance of Christ Jesus they will react to you differently. Here is where the major trimming begins. This is where and when you will find out who really are your 'friends'. Not all family members will rally around you or be so understanding and supportive of your decision. You will be criticized, ridiculed, mocked and betrayed by some of these very people whom you thought would always have your back. This is where God begins to trim and cut away from your life the things and people He wants to remove from your life. Have no doubt that this is going to be hard but this is so that you will have a better outcome. Remember what verse 2 says, any Believer/Christian that does not endure the consequence [that stops enduring] He cuts away. Stay in the word and pray constantly. Not everyone is meant to partake in your new life in Christ.

Live in Me and I will live in you. Live in God through His Word and prayer. Attend church, Bible studies and any other avenues that will keep you close to God. You cannot endure the consequence on your own without abiding in Jesus. You must be essentially united to Jesus. Seek My face [inquire for and require My Presence as your vital need (your most important need). (Ps. 27:8) Jesus is the Vine and we are the branches on the vine. Apart from Jesus we will be cut off and can do nothing. We wither and eventually die. As we live and abide in Him we will have an abundant outcome. No believer can produce his own results. If you do not dwell in Him you will be broken off and thrown out and will wither and die. Then the day will come and you will be gathered up and thrown into the fire. This is the day of judgment, you will be thrown into an eternal hell. Hell is for real, do not take it lightly. It is not a myth.

If you live in Jesus and stay vitally united to Him and His words remain in you and He continues to live in your heart, ask whatever you will, and it shall be done for you.

When you endure the consequence, to have more and excellent result, God the Father is honored and glorified, and you show and prove yourselves to be the true followers of God.

Jesus loves you just as the Father Loved Him. So continue to abide in God's Love through Jesus.

If you keep His commandments and continue to obey His instructions, you will live in His love and live on in it just as Jesus obeyed His Father's commandments and live on in His love.

Jesus came to tell us these things so that His joy and delight will be in us and so that our joy and gladness will be of full measure and complete and overflowing.—Delight yourself in the Lord, and He will give you the desires and secret petitions of your heart.—(Psalms 37:4)

So what is the commandment? That you love one another just as I, Jesus, loves you. There is no greater love. No one has shown a greater or stronger love for us than Jesus. He laid down His life for us His friends. We are His friends if we continue to do as He commands us to do. We are no longer servants. When we were sinners we were slaves to sin. No one who is a child of God is any longer a slave. Jesus told us everything that His Father told Him, how we should live and how we should love. We are not servants, for a servant does not know what his master is doing. We are His friends, friends tell their friends everything. Jesus told us everything that He learned from His Father. He has chosen us and equipped us so that we will and can endure the outcome and keep on enduring that our result may be eternal. That it may remain and abide so that whatever we ask the Father in Jesus' name [as presenting all that I AM-*as gifting all because I EXIST*] He will give it to us.

Again what is the command? THAT YOU LOVE ONE ANOTHER!

When the world hates you, know that it hated Jesus before it hated you. You made the decision to separate from the world and the things of the world. When you participate in the things and matters of the world, the world will accept you or treat you as its own. You do not follow after the world any longer but because God has chosen you out of the world, the world will hate you.

Remember that I told you that a Christian is not greater than his Master. A Christian does what he is told to do. He is a Christian commissioned to do his Master's bidding.—Matthew 28:19-20 . . . ." Go therefore and make disciples of all people, baptizing them in the name of the Father and of the Son and of the Holy Spirit, teaching them to abide by all things that I have commanded you; and look, I am with you always, even to the end of the age. Amen! (So be it!)—If the Master was harassed and oppressed, they will also harass and oppress the Christian. If the

Christian kept the Minister's word and obeyed the Minister's teaching, your Christian student will also keep and obey your teachings.

The world will do all this to you. They will cause you to suffer because you profess the name of Jesus and because they do not know and understand the God who sent Jesus.

If I, Jesus, had not come and spoken to them (the Jews), they would not be guilty of sin. They would be blameless but now they (the world *Romans 2:29*) have no excuse for their sin. Exodus 19-20

Whoever hates Jesus also hates God the Father.

If Jesus had not completed in their midst the works and miracles no one else had ever done, the world would not be guilty of sin. But the fact now is that they have seen these works and have hated and still hates both Jesus and God The Father. Everywhere you turn today you see a church or on the television, the internet, the advertisements about God or an invitation to church. It is impossible for many people to say today that they have not heard of God or of Jesus. At times I hand out tracts and just as many people take them as those who do not. I've noticed those who do not take them sometimes has this look on their face as if to say if I don't take it I can say I didn't know. Little do they know that they will be reminded that an opportunity was given them and they refused.

But this is to be so that the word written in their Law might be fulfilled, "They hated Jesus without a cause."

But when the Holy Spirit comes Whom I will send to you from the Father, the Spirit of Truth who comes from the Father, He [Himself] will testify regarding Me.

But you also will testify and be My witnesses, because you have been with Me from the beginning.

Before Jesus came and began His ministry, there was only the Ten Commandments and the Jewish Laws to abide by. We have Jesus from

41

the beginning because we asked Him to come into our hearts on faith believing. So Jesus is with us from the beginning of our new life.

John 16:12-15; 22-24; 27-28; 33; 30-31

I still have many things to say to you, but you are not able to carry them or take them on you or understand them now.

But when He the Holy Spirit of Truth comes, He will guide you into all reality; for He will not speak on His own authority or His own message. He will tell whatever He hears from the Father He will declare and reveal to you about the things that will happen in the future.

The Holy Spirit will honor and glorify Jesus. He will draw upon what is Jesus' and will declare and transmit it to you.

Everything that God the Father has is Jesus'. That is what Jesus meant when He said the Holy Spirit will take the things that are Jesus' and will reveal it to you.

So for the time being you also will be in distress; but Jesus will see you again. The trouble, trials and distresses of the world are only for a moment so don't be distressed, don't cave in to depression about them. You will see Jesus and your hearts will rejoice and no one can take your joy away.

And when you see Jesus again you will not need to ask anything of Him. All your questions will be answered. While here and now we are battling to gain understanding of this reality (1 Corinthians 13:12) once we see Jesus there will be no need to ask Him any questions. Jesus convinces us with solemn certainty that His Father will grant whatever you ask *as gifting all because I EXIST*. Up to this time you have not asked a [single] thing in My Name [*as gifting all because I EXIST*]; so now ask and keep asking so that your joy may be filled.

The Heavenly Father loves us because we love Jesus and we believe that Jesus came from the Heavenly Father above.

Jesus came from the Father into this world for a time and He left this world to return to His Father but will come again.

With this knowledge we now can have perfect peace and confidence which Jesus gave to us before He left. As long as we are here in this world we will have worries, sufferings and torment but be of good cheer. Take courage in the gift of peace He left us and the confidence of His love and protection over you. Jesus overcame the world and so can we. He took away its power to harm us and has already conquered if for us. All we have to do is follow the commands He has left us.

Now we believe and we are equipped with all the information we need and have no need to ask any questions. For we are now sure that Jesus came from God the Father.

Jesus answered them, Do you now believe? Do you believe at last?

The Consequence
So for the present you are also in sorrow (in distress and depressed); In the world you have tribulations and trials and distress and frustrations; I have told you these things so that you should not be offended (taken unawares and falter, or be caused to stumble and fall away). [I told you to keep you from being scandalized and repelled. If the world hates you, know that it hated Me before it hated you. If you belonged to the world, the world would treat you with affection and would love you as its own. But because you are not of the world [no longer one of it], but I have chosen (selected) you out of the world, the world hates and (detests) you.

The Outcome
But be of good cheer [take courage; be confident, certain, undaunted]. For I have overcome the world. [I have deprived it of power to harm you and have conquered it for you]. Dear little children, I am to be with you only a little longer. Just a little while now, and the world will not see Me anymore, but you will see Me; because I live, you will also live.

The Result
In My Father's house there are many dwelling places (homes). If it were not so, I would not have told you; for I am going to prepare a place for

you, and when I go and make ready a place for you, I will come again and will take you to Myself, that where I am you may be also. And [to the place] where I am going, you know the way. I am the way, the truth and the Life. No one comes to the Father (God) except by Me (Jesus). But I will see you and then your hearts will rejoice; and [then] no one can take your joy.

These passages were taken from John 15 and 16

THE ULTIMATE ACT OF LOVE

For God so greatly loved and dearly prized the world that He [even] gave up the only begotten (unique) Son, so that whoever believes in (trusts in, clings to, relies on) Him shall not perish (come to destruction, be lost) but have eternal (everlasting) life. John 3:16

Matthew 26:36-46
Jesus knew what he was facing that night when He went to pray in the Garden of Gethsemane. He took with Him Peter, James and John. As He began to be sorrowful and deeply disturbed He told them; "My soul is exceedingly sorrowful, even to death. Stay here and watch with me." Then He went further into the garden to pray and this is what He prayed: "O My Father, if it is possible, let this cup pass from Me; nevertheless, not as I will, but as you will" . . . . and again He prayed, "O My Father, if this cup cannot pass away from Me unless I drink it, Your will be done". Jesus meant it. When you pray to the Heavenly Father, Your will be done, do you mean it? Jesus suffered! He was crucified. He died and rose again from the grave for all of us.

Hebrews 10:1-10
For since the Law was merely a rough plan (suggesting) of the good things to come—instead of fully expressing those things—it can never by offering the same atoning continually year after year make perfect those who approach [its altars].

For if it were otherwise, would [these atonements] not have stopped being offered? Since the worshipers had once for all been cleansed, they would no longer have any guilt or consciousness of sin.

But [as it is] these sacrifices annually bring a fresh remembrance of sins [to be atoned for].

Because the blood of bulls and goats is powerless to take sins away.

Therefore, when He [Christ] entered into the world, He said, Sacrifices and offerings You (Father) have not desired, but instead You have made ready a body for Me [to offer];

In burnt offerings and sin offerings You have taken no delight.

Then I said, Behold, here I am coming to do your will, O God (My Father)—[to fulfill] what is written of Me in the Volume of the Book.

When He said just before, You have neither desired, nor have You taken delight in sacrifices and offerings and burnt offerings and sin offerings— all of which are offered according to the Law—

He went on to say, Behold [here] I am, coming to do Your will. Thus He does away and voids the first (former) order [as a means of making amends for sin] so that He might introduce and establish the second (latter) order.

And in accordance with this will [of God], we have been made holy (consecrated and sanctified) through the offering made once for all of the body of Jesus Christ (the Anointed One).

Jesus became the perfect sacrifice for our sins, iniquities, sicknesses and diseases so that we may have eternal life with Him and the Father all because He loves us so much.

LOVE IN ACTION

1 John 3:11-24

For this is the message (the announcement) which you have heard from the first, that we should love one another,

[And] not be like Cain who [took his nature and got his motivation] from the evil one and slew his brother. And why did he slay him? Because his deeds (activities, works) were wicked and malicious and his brother's were righteous (virtuous).

Do not be surprised and wonder, brethren, that the world detests and pursues you with hatred.

We know that we have passed over out of death into Life by the fact that we love the brethren (our fellow Christians). He who does not love abides (remains, is held and kept continually) in [spiritual] death.

Anyone who hates (abominates, detests) his brother [in Christ] is [at heart] a murderer, and you know that no murderer has eternal life abiding (persevering) within him.

By this we come to know (progressively to recognize, to perceive, to understand) the [essential] love: that He laid down His [own] life for us; and we ought to lay [our] lives down for [those who are our] brothers [in Him].

But if anyone has this world's goods (resources for sustaining life) and he sees his brother and fellow believer in need, yet closes his heart of compassion against him, how can the love of God live and remain in him?

Little children, let us not love [merely] in theory or in speech but in deed and in truth (in practice and in sincerity).

Marcella A. Spence

By this we shall come to know and (perceive recognize, and understand) that we are of the Truth and can reassure (quiet, conciliate, and pacify) our hearts in His presence,

Whenever our hearts in [tormenting] self-accusation make us feel guilty and condemn us. [For we are in God's hands.] For He is above and greater than our consciences (our hearts), and He knows (perceives and understands) everything [nothing is hidden from Him].

And, beloved, if our consciences (our hearts) do not accuse us [if they do not make us feel guilty and condemn us], we have confidence (complete assurance and boldness) before God,

And we receive from Him whatever we ask, because we [watchfully] obey His orders [observe His suggestions and injunctions, follow His plan for us] and [habitually] practice what is pleasing to Him.

And this is His order (His command, His injunction): that we should believe in (put our faith and trust in and adhere to and rely on) the name of His Son Jesus Christ (the Messiah), and that we should love one another, just as He has commanded us.

All who keep His commandments [who obey] His orders and follow His plan, live and continue to live, to stay and abide in Him, and He in them. [They let Christ be a home to them and they are the home of Christ.] And by this we know and understand and have the proof that He [really] lives and makes His home in us: by the [Holy] Spirit Whom He has given us.

LOVE IN ACTION
TRANSLATED

For this is the message (the announcement) which you have heard from the first, that we should love one another.

And be not like Cain who took his basic character and got his motivation from the evil one and killed his brother. And why did he kill Abel? Basic jealousy, because Abel's offering was accepted by God. Cain brought the Lord an offering of the first fruit of the ground. According to Arthur W. Pink, "Gleanings in Genesis"—In bringing the offering he did, Cain denied that he was a sinful creature under the sentence of divine condemnation. He insisted on approaching God on the ground of personal worthiness. Instead, of accepting God's way, He offered to God the fruits of the ground which God had cursed. He presented the product of his own toil, the work of his own hands and God refused it. {As taken from the footnotes of the Amplified Bible.} Be careful saints, jealousy can creep into your soul like a snake slithers in for the attack, silently. These strikes of jealousy can be swift and lethal. Some strikes kill and some maim. In Song of Solomon 8:6 the Shulamite said to her beloved so as not to forget her: Set me like a brand upon your heart, like a seal (tattoo) upon your arm; for love is as strong as death,—death is [4]inevitable-*incapable of being avoided or prevented*. Spiritual death is inevitable to the natural man, the person who has never accepted Christ. Physical death is inevitable to some of us of this present day generation. There will be some who will not experience this physical death. Believer be aware that we too do not experience a spiritual death. So once God's love is in you it brings on to you all the qualities of God, that is inevitable . . . the verse goes on to say jealousy is hard and cruel as Sheol (the place of the dead) this a particular level in hell, its flashes are flashes of fire,—a most [4]vehement-*vigorous, forceful, intense*—flame [the very flame of the Lord]. Deuteronomy 4:24 says, For the Lord your God is a consuming fire, a jealous God. A consuming fire is a fire that destroys completely, yet in hell you remain alive in this consuming fire. This is not a place where you want to spend eternity. So be very careful saints, jealousy will lead to your spiritual death. It can also led to physical death.

Do not be surprised and wonder brethren, that the world detests and pursues you with hatred. John 15:18 says if the world hates you, know that it hated Me before it hated you. Blessed are you when men hate you and when they exclude you, and revile you, and cast out your name as evil for the Son of Man's sake. Luke 6:22(NKJV) We know that we have passed over out of death into Life by the fact that we love the brethren (our fellow Christians). With this understanding, we have come to know the indispensible Love of Christ. Just as Christ laid down His life for us, we too ought to lay down our life for our fellow brethren in Christ. He who does not love is held and kept continually in [spiritual] death. Anyone who hates his brethren in Christ is at heart a murderer, and you know that no murderer has eternal life abiding, within him.

But if anyone has this world's resources for sustaining life and sees his brother and fellow believer in need, yet closes his heart of compassion against him, how can the love of God live and remain in him? Fellow Christians let us not love merely in assuming or in vain talk but in action and in truth (in practice and sincerity).

By this we shall come to know (understand) that we are of the Truth of Jesus Christ. In John 14:6 Jesus says, I am the Way-*means, manner of living. He has set the example as to how we think and react.* the Truth-*Reality* and the Life-*the manner of living.* Jesus is our Way/ means. How? He provides, protects, comforts plus more. He's the true Reality of what is and what will be. True Perfection and Excellence-I AM. *(Go back and read verse 12 of 'The Way of Love Translated'.)* The Life-That belief of belonging from Which (the One that) gave the breath of Life-Genesis 2:7, from Which (the One that) makes it possible to have the Bread of Life-John 6:41,48, and the Water of Life-Revelations 22:1, 17, from Which we live and have our being-Acts 17:28a for growth and energy for strength. (Hebrews 4:12) *The manner of living is given to us throughout the New Testament.* On accord of this, we can be assured our hearts are quiet in His presence whenever our hearts in tormenting, making us feel guilty and condemning us. For we are in God's hands. For He is above and greater than our hearts and He knows everything and nothing is hidden from Him. And, beloved, if (our heart) does not accuse us to make us feel guilty and or condemn us, then we have a complete assurance and boldness before God. And we will receive from Him whatever we ask because we watchfully obey His orders, pay attention to His suggestions and commands, follow His plans for us and habitually practice what is pleasing to Him.

And this is His command: that we should believe in, put our faith and trust in, obey and rely on the name of His Son, Jesus Christ and that we should love one another just as He has commanded us to do. All who keep His Commands abides in Him and He in them. We are to let Christ be a home to us and so are we to be a home to Christ. And by this we know and understand and have the evidence that He really lives and makes His home in us by the Holy Spirit Whom He has given us. Amen. (So be it.)

WHERE DID LOVE START?

(Genesis 1:21, 25, 31)

When God created the heavens and the earth He already had a plan. That plan included you and me. Remember, God is omniscient-*all knowing*. He knows how many times you will blink your eyes in your lifetime before you are even a thought.

God wanted a different kind of worship. Though He had sons (angels) (Job 1:6) that worshiped Him always, they did so because they were created to do so. They were expected to love, worship, adore and obey Him. What He now wanted was someone who <u>chose</u> to worship Him. To love, worship, adore and obey Him because that is what they truly want to do.

When He created Man He gave him instructions of what to do and <u>not</u> to do. If God didn't want man to choose He would not have put the tree there with instructions. It would have been easier to leave it out of the Garden. He also put man on the same planet where He sent Lucifer. Selah. (Pause and think on that) There is no good without bad and vice versa. Remember, God is omniscient-*all knowing*. God knew before He created man that he was going to fall. That man would disobey his creator's command. He knew that He (God) Himself would have to rescue man from themselves. That's the whole point people! God loved us before we existed. God loves us so much that He created the means through Which (the One that) He would show us how much he loves us. He became one of us. He became His Son to rescue us from sin. How awesome is that?

Man had God's command to obey (Genesis 2:9, 16-17) and we know the choice that was made. (Gen. 3:6) By that choice nakedness-*awareness of wrong doing* fell upon man. Genesis 3:8-10 is only three verses but these three verses gave a novel of information about God and the relationship that God and man developed in the Garden of Eden. God came into the Garden of Eden in the cool of the day, every day. In the cool of the day, after Adam had tended to the garden and the animals. I'm sure their conversations were about all that Adam experienced each day. I'm also sure that God was instructing Adam on how to care for the earth and the animals and of course, Eve. God never gives a task without instructions. Notice the verse says, "And they heard the sound of the Lord God walking in the Garden in the cool of the day." This was customary. [When God is near, He can be heard and His presence is felt.] They were familiar with the sounds and presence of God. This was the time when God communed with man and this is where love developed. Gen. 1:31— And God saw every fellowship that He made, and behold, it was good (suitable, pleasant) and He approved it completely.

Before Adam's disobedience all was pleasant. There was no fear, no hiding or no nakedness. Where there is love [God's Love], there is no fear or reason to hide. (1 John 4:18) Where there is love there is no sin. This was the first time God came into the garden and had to call out to Adam. Verse 9, But the Lord called to Adam and said to him, "Where are you?" All the other times they heard God come into the garden and just as God was eager to commune with them, they were also eager to commune with God. He was their Father, He formed and gave them life. They knew that. Today was different, they were afraid to see Him, they were hiding. Something had changed. Disobedience had exposed their natural nature. They were no longer enveloped in God's Love and glory. Sin was present in the Garden of Eden. When sin is present there is <u>always</u> an awareness of it no matter how much you try to deny its presence. Disobedience brings on sin and love becomes invalid. Sin cancels love. Where God's love abide, sin does not abide. Thanks to God by the time Adam and Eve left the Garden their sin was already forgiven. The first sacrifice for forgiveness of sin was made by the Most High Priest in the Garden of Eden.

To love, worship, adore and obey God is your choice. Where you spend eternity is also your choice.

THE SOURCE OF LOVE

1 John 4:7-21

Beloved, let us love one another, for love is (springs) from God; and he who loves [his fellowmen] is begotten (born) of God and is coming [progressively] to know and understand God [to perceive and recognize and get better and clearer knowledge of Him].

He who does not love has not become acquainted with God [does not and never did know Him], for God is love.

In this the love of God was made manifest (displayed) where we are concerned: in that God sent His Son, the only begotten or unique [Son], into the world so that we might live through Him.

In this is love: not that we loved God, but that He loved us and sent His Son to be the propitiation (the atoning sacrifice) for our sins.

Beloved, if God loved us so [very much], we also ought to love one another.

No man has at any time [yet] seen God. But if we love one another, God abides (lives and remains) in us and His love (that love which is essentially His) is brought to completion (to its full maturity, runs its full course, is perfected) in us!

By this we come to know (perceive, recognize, and understand) that we abide (live and remain) in Him and He in us: because He has given (in parted) to us of His [Holy] Spirit.

And [besides] we ourselves have seen (have deliberately and steadfastly contemplated) and bear witness that the Father has sent the Son [as the] Savior of the world.

Anyone who confesses (acknowledges, owns) that Jesus is the Son of God, God abides (lives, makes His home) in him and he [abides, lives, makes his home] in God.

And we know (understand, recognize, are conscious of, by observation and by experience) and believe (adhere to and put faith in and rely on) the love God cherishes for us. God is love, and he who dwells and continues in love dwells and continues in God, and God dwells and continues in him.

In this [union and communion with Him] love is brought to completion and attains perfection with us, that we may have confidence for the day of judgment [with assurance and boldness to face Him], because as He is, so are we in this world.

There is no fear in love [dread does not exist], but full-grown (complete, perfect) love turns fear out of doors and expels every trace of terror! For fear brings the thought of punishment, and [so] he who is afraid has not reached the full maturity of love [is not yet grown into love's complete perfection].

We love Him, because He first loved us.

If anyone says, I love God, and hates (detests, abominates) his brother [in Christ], he is a liar; for he who does not love his brother, whom he has seen, cannot love God, Whom he has not seen.

And this command (charge, order, injunction) we have from Him: that he who loves God shall love his brother [Believer] also.

THE SOURCE OF LOVE TRANSLATED

God is and should be your only source of love. The definition of source is one who supplies your information. When it comes to love, God is the <u>only true source</u>.

So Beloved, let us love one another, for love it comes into existence from God and he who loves his fellowman is born again in God and is continuing in stages to know and understand God. To perceive and recognize and get a better and clearer knowledge of Him. However, you have to read His Word in order to get to know Him better.

He who does not love has not become familiar with God. He does not and never did know Him for God is Love. In this the love of God was known—John 3:16—in that God sent His only begotten—*beget through human form-Mary,* unique Son into this world so that you might live by the manner of living of Him. In this is love: not your love for God but His Love for you why He sent His Son to be the atoning sacrifice for your sins. Beloved, if God loved you so much, you should also love one another.

No man has at any time yet seen God, but if you love one another, God lives and remains in you and His love, that love which is originally His—*of His Spirit,* is brought to completion, to its full maturity and is perfected in you! By this you will come to recognize and understand that you can live and remain in Him and He in you; because He has given to you His [Holy] Spirit. And besides yourselves have heard and have read His Word that the Father has sent His Son as the Savior of the world.

Thus anyone who acknowledges and owns that Jesus is the Son of God, God will make His home in him and he will make his home in God. And he will understand and recognize and become conscious of by observation and by experience and believe and put your faith in and rely on the love God cherishes for you. God is love, and he who dwells and continues in love dwells and continues in God, and God dwells and continues in him. In this union and communion with God, love is brought to completion and attains perfection with you, that you may have confidence and boldness to face Him, because as He is, so are we in this world.

There is no fear in love, fear does not exist but complete and perfect love turns fear out of doors and drives out every trace of terror! For fear brings with it the thought of punishment, and so he who is afraid has not fully developed in love, is not yet grown into loves' complete perfection.

You love God because He first loved you.

If anyone says, I love God and hates his brother in Christ, he is a liar; for he who does not love his brother in Christ whom he has seen cannot love God whom he has not seen.

And this command you have from God: He who loves God shall love His Christian brother also.

LOVE EVERLASTING

Romans 8: 35-39

Who shall ever separate us form Christ's love? Shall suffering and affliction and tribulation? Or calamity and distress? Or persecution or hunger or destitution or peril or sword?

Even as it is written, For Thy sake we are put to death all the daylong; we are regarded and counted as sheep for the slaughter.

Yet amid all these things we are more that conquerors and gain a surpassing victory through Him who loved us.

For I am persuaded beyond doubt (am sure) that neither death nor life, nor angels nor principalities, nor things impending and threatening nor things to come, nor powers,

Nor height nor depth, nor anything else in all creation will be able to separate us from the love of God which is in Christ Jesus our Lord.

LOVE EVERLASTING
TRANSLATED

Who shall be able to separate us from Christ's Love? Shall suffering-*the bearing of pain or distress* and affliction-*any cause of suffering* and tribulation-*great misery or distress or the cause of it*? Or calamity-*great disasters* and distress-*a state of danger or trouble*? Or persecution-*to afflict constantly so as to injure or distress* or hunger-*discomfort caused by the need for food* or destitution-*totally made poor* or peril-*something that may cause harm* or sword-*war*? At this present moment you can say no but there is coming a day very soon when these things will be put to the test. When Jesus comes and take the church, those who have been living according to the Word of God and are ready. What will become of those who are left behind? There will be sufferings, afflictions, great trials, calamities, distresses, danger, war, hunger and utter lack. Will you be ready and willing to die for Christ's sake? The verse says . . . .

Even as it is written, For Thy (Christ) sake we are put to death all the daylong; we are regarded and counted as sheep for the slaughter. Matthew 10:22—And you will be hated by all for My Name's sake, but he who perseveres and endures to the end <u>will be saved</u> [from spiritual disease and death in the world to come]. This is the outcome—the abundant fruit—the result.

Yet amid all these thing we are more than conquerors and gain a surpassing victory through Him Who loves us.

For I am persuaded beyond doubt-*am sure*, that neither death not life, nor angels nor *principalities—*top ranking demonic beings, they are chief demons which correspond with archangels among the holy angels. They hold sway (influence) over the souls of people. A principality is what assigns demonic spirits to operate in disobedience. They also rule over continents and nations. These demons are subject to Christ and spirit-filled believers. (Eph 2:6)* nor things impending-*to come* and threatening nor things to come, nor *powers-*the next level of evil officers of darkness. The word powers come from the greek word exousia which means delegated authority like that of a policeman. These powers are subject to Christ.* Nor height-*extreme* nor depth-*intensity* nor anything else will be able to separate you from the Love of God which is in Christ Jesus our Lord.

Why is it Christ Jesus? Jesus said to him, I am the Way, the Truth and the Life; no one comes to the Father except through Me. John 14:6

For God so greatly loves and dearly prizes the world that He [even] gave up His only begotten (unique) Son, so that whoever believes in (trusts in, clings to, relies on) Him shall not perish (come to destruction, be lost) but have eternal (everlasting) life. John 3:16

He who believes in (has faith in, clings to, relies on) the Son now possesses eternal life. Whoever disobeys (is unbelieving toward, refuses to trust in, disregards, is not subject to) the Son will never see (experience) life, but [instead] the wrath of God abides on him. [God's displeasure remains on Him; His indignation hangs over him continually.] John 3:36

P

O

E

M

S

BY
MARCELLA A. SPENCE

WHAT IS LOVE?

Love is the Law
You're to worship only Me. (Ex. 20:2-6)
Love is the command
You're all one family. (John 13:34)

Love is a gift (1 Cor. 13:31)
It was given for free.
Just cling to, rely on
There's eternal life in Me. (Jn. 3:16)

Love never hungers
I am the Bread of Life
Love never thirsts
Just give Me your life. (Jn. 6:35)

Love is the Way
The Truth and the Life.
You won't meet My Father
If you continue in strife. Jn. 14:6)

Love guides and protects
There is nothing to fear. (Jn. 10:7-11)
Love is the Light
Follow me, I'll take you there. (Jn. 8:12)

Love is the vine each
Branch trimmed and clipped. (Jn. 15:1-5)
Love's the fruit of the Spirit
The rest is lost without it. (Gal. 5:22-23)

Love was crucified (Jn. 19:18)
Love has conquered death.
Now Love is alive (Matt. 28:6)
And Love is glorified. (Lk. 24:51)

Love is your choice
Obey My command.
Abide in Our Love
Welcome home to heaven.

God is Love!
Love is a person!
Love is God!
Love is not an emotion!

Marcella A. Spence

LOVE

Love comes into existence
From the creator of Life,
Loves dwells in a heart
That has distance from strife.

In Love there is hope,
Joy, peace and faith.
Love brings comfort and security
To a place where dwells hate.

Love is a miracle
Handle it with care.
Just one act of selfishness
And Love will disappear.

Don't take Love for granted
It may not return.
In the way once given
But still, Love never fails.

Marcella A. Spence

GOD LOVES YOU

He maketh the sun
To rise on your troubles,
He maketh the wind
To blow on your face.

He wraps His loving
Arms around you,
As He carries you
Through strife and pain.

He guides your every footstep
When you know not where to go.
He holds your hand
And leads you to dry land.

He builds you up
When life breaks you down.
He puts a smile on your face
When He sees a frown.

So hold your head up high
He's standing at your side,
Take courage dear child
For in Him you can hide.

Marcella A. Spence

PRAYER OF GRACE

I love you Lord with all I have
Because you are the Lord My God.
I will love my neighbor and enemies too
Making it a practice will not be hard to do.

I pray for them and invoke upon them blessings
Though they scandalize my character and name.
Lord bless them and draw them close to you
It is written, they can bring me no shame.

Though they take all I have from me
Bless me, that I may bless the needy and poor.
I'll treat them as I want to be treated
Bless me, that I may bless them even more.

May I lend and expect no return
Help me to give, considering it no loss.
Help me to forget what they have taken
Please help me to be merciful and count not the cost.

Marcella A. Spence

BENEDICTION

Ephesians 4:15-21

Dear Father:
For Whom every family in heaven and on earth is named. From Whom all fatherhood takes its title and derives its name.

May you grant me out of the rich treasury of your glory to be strengthened and reinforced with mighty power in my inner being by the Holy Spirit. Yourself in my innermost being and personality!

May Christ through my faith actually dwell (settle down, abide, make His permanent home) in my heart. May I be rooted deep in Your Love, grounded securely on Your Love,

That I may have the power to be strong to get the meaning and know and believe with all the saints, God's devoted people, the experience of His Love. What is the lack of restriction in great detail and extreme and intensity of Your Love;

That I may come to know with regard to use through experience for myself the Love of Christ, which by far goes beyond mere knowledge [without experience]; that toward all the abundance of God I may have all the ample esteem of the divine Presence and become wholly filled and flooded with God Himself.

Now by the action of his power that is at work within me, is able to carry out His purpose and do super abundantly, far over and above all that I dare ask or think, without bounds beyond my highest prayers, desires, thoughts, hopes or dreams—

To God be the glory in the church and in Christ Jesus throughout all generations forever and ever. Amen. (So be it.)

EPILOGUE

Grace and spiritual peace be yours from God
our Father and the Lord Jesus Christ.
May blessing be to the God who has blessed us
in Christ in the heavenly realm.

In His Love God chose us, picked us out Himself
as His own (Gen. 1:27-*created*) in Christ (Gen. 2:7-*formed*)
that we should be holy and blameless
in His sight before Him in Love. (John 3:16)

For God planned in love for us (Romans 5:8) to be revealed
as His own children through Jesus Christ (Rom. 8:15-17)
according to the purpose of His will (Rom. 8:28-30)
to the praise and care of His Grace
which God so freely bestowed on us in Jesus (Ephesians 2:8)

In Jesus we have redemption through His blood,
forgiveness of our shortcoming and trespasses in harmony and unity
with the riches and the generosity of His Grace. (Ephesians 2:8)
Which He marked upon us in every kind of wisdom
and understanding, making known to us the secret of His will.

And it is this: In harmony and unity with good pleasure
which He had previously settled and set forth in Jesus.
In Jesus we also were made God's heirs and we gained
possession of an inheritance; for we have been
predestined in harmony and unity with His goal,
who works out everything in harmony and balance
with the guidance and plan of His own will.

So that we who first put our confidence in Jesus have been
destined and appointed to live for the praise of His glory!
In Jesus you also have heard the word of Truth,
the Gospel of your salvation, believed in and

obeyed and relied on Him and
we are stamped with the seal of the Holy Spirit.
The Spirit is the down payment of our heirship,
in hope of its full redemption and our taking
complete possession of it to the praise of His Glory.

And so that you can know and understand what is
the immeasurable and unlimited and exceeding greatness
of God's power in and for who believe as shown
in the working of His mighty strength. For it is by
free grace that you are saved through your faith.

And this salvation is not of yourselves but it is the gift of God.
Not because of the fulfillment of the Law's demands,
lest any man should boast. It is not the result
of what anyone can possibly do, so no one can
pride himself in it or the glory in himself.
(Ephesians 1:1-9, 11-14, 19; 2:8-9)

REVERE GOD AND GIVE HIM GLORY!! (Revelations 14:7)

The hope of the un-conforming upright is delight,
but the hope of the wicked
—those who are out of harmony with God
—comes to nothing. (Proverbs 10:28)

GLOSSARY

A

⁴abide(s) (ing) . . . . 2. to remain: stay 3. to dwell: sojourn

⁵abominates . . . . 1. to hate; loathe 2. to dislike very much

⁵abundance(t) . . . . a great supply; more than enough

⁴adhere . . . . 1. to stick fast or together: cling 2. to support or be devoted to 3. to carry something out without deviation

⁴affection . . . . a fond or tender feeling toward another

⁴antiquated . . . . out of date: obsolete

apodictic laws . . . . laws that cannot be broken, there are no exceptions when it comes to the obedience of the law. (Those that began "Thou shalt not.")

⁴arrogant . . . . overbearing and self-important: haughty

⁴assurance . . . . 1. a statement intended to inspire confidence: guarantee 2a. certainty b) self-confidence

¹atonement . . . . reconciliation—the process by which God and man can once again become "at-one"

⁵authority . . . . the power or right to command, act, etc.

B

⁴being . . . . 1. existence 2. one that lives 3. one's basic or essential nature; essence

⁴boastful . . . . to talk in a self-admiring way: brag

⁵brethren . . . . brothers: now chiefly religious)those who have professed the same faith)

⁵brother . . . . 3. fellow member of the same race, church, profession, etc.

C

⁵calamity . . . . a great misfortune; disaster

⁴calloused . . . . 2. insensitive: unfeeling

casuistic laws . . . . case by case laws which is applied to specific situations (example: Deut. 25:1-3)

¹command . . . . to order or direct with authority

¹commandment . . . . a command or mandate

¹conceited . . . . an exaggerated estimate of one's own importance

⁵concise . . . . brief and to the point; short and clear

⁵conspicuous . . . . 1. easy to see

⁴contemplated . . . . to consider as possible: intended

⁴covenant . . . . a binding agreement: compact

D
[4]**dwell** .... 1. to live as an inhabitant: reside 3a. to focus one's attention

E
[4]**earnestly** .... characterized by showing deep sincerity: serious
[5]**eminent** .... 3. renowned; distinguished 4. outstanding
[5]**emotion** .... 1. strong feeling
[5]**emotional** .... 1. of or showing emotion
[4]**endure**(s) (ing) .... 1.to carry on through: undergo successfully 2. to
    tolerate: bear
[4]**enigma** .... 1. a riddle 2. a perplexing or baffling matter, person, etc.
[4]**envious** .... feeling, showing or marked by envy
[4]**essence** .... 1. the properties of a thing (person) that makes it what it is
    fundamental nature—(personality, character) 2. the most important
    element 3.a concentrate-*focus* of a substance (spiritual focus)
[5]**expiate**(ing) .... to make amend for (wrongdoing or guilt); atone for

F
[5]**fragmentary** .... consisting of fragments; not complete
[4]**fundamental** .... 1a. essential: basic b. of major significance: central

H
[5]**haughty** (ily) .... having or showing great pride in one self and
    contempt for others; arrogant

I
[5]**idolatry** .... excessive reverence for or devotion to a person or thing
[5]**in part** .... partly-*not fully or completely*
[4]**iniquity** .... 1. wickedness: sinfulness 2. a grossly immoral act: sin
    (passed down from generation to generation Exo. 20:5)
[4]**injustice** .... 1. violation of justice or another's rights: unfairness
[5]**invoke** .... 1. to call on (God, the Muses, etc.) for blessings, help, etc.

J
[5]**just** .... 2. righteous [a just man] 3. deserved [just praise] 4. lawful
[5]**justify** (ied) .... to show to be just, right, etc. 2. Theology—to free
    from blame or guilt

L

⁴the Law . . . . 3. the body of precepts that express the divine will as set forth in the Old Testament

⁵live (ing) . . . . 1. to have life 2a. to remain alive b) to endure **vt.**-1. to carry out in one's life [to live one's faith]

M

⁵manifest . . . . apparent to the senses or the mind; obvious **vt.**-to show plainly; reveal

⁵maxim . . . . a concise rule of conduct

⁵means . . . . 1. that by which something is obtained; agency [source of travel] 2. resources; wealth

⁵merciful . . . . having or showing mercy; compassionate; lenient

⁵mercy . . . . 1. a refraining from harming offenders, enemies, etc. 3. a disposition to be forgiving or be kind 4. the power to forgive

⁵monotheism . . . . the belief that there is only one God

O

⁵obsolete . . . . 1. no longer in use 2. out-of-date

P

⁵partiality . . . . 1. favoring one person, faction etc. more than another; biased

⁴perish . . . . to become ruined, spoiled or destroyed: die

⁵persecute (tion) . . . . to afflict constantly so as to injure or distress, as for reasons of religion, race, etc.

⁴persevere (ing) . . . . to persist in an idea, purpose, or task despite obstacles

⁵polytheism . . . . belief in more one god

⁵power . . . . n.1. ability to so or act **vt.**-to supply with a source of power. (unwaveringly)

*powers . . . . the next level of evil officers of darkness. The word powers come from the greek word exousia which means delegated authority like that of a policeman. These powers are subject to Christ.—*from Everyone's Guide to Demons & Spiritual by Ron Phillips*

⁵precepts . . . . a rule of moral conduct; maxim

⁵preeminent . . . . eminent above others; surpassing

pride .... excessive self-esteem: conceit

*****principalities** .... 1. the territories ruled by a prince 2. top ranking demonic beings, chief demons who hold sway over the souls of people—*from Everyone's Guide to Demons & Spiritual by Ron Phillips*

prominent .... immediately noticeable: conspicuous 3. widely known and esteemed

pronouncement .... a formed statement, as of an opinion

property (ies) .... 2a. characteristic traits, quality or attributes

propitiation .... that which appeases or makes atonement (see atonement)

prune 2 (s) .... 1. to cut or trim 2. to remove unnecessary and unwanted parts (issues, situations, and behaviors in our lives)

pure .... 2. free from impurities and contaminants 4. free from faults; sinless

purify (ies) (ed) .... to make or become clean or pure

R

reality .... 1. the quality or state of being actual or true 2. one that is real 3. .the totality of all existing things

reconciliation .... the bringing together of God and man in union of peace. This reconciliation was brought about by the work of Jesus in the flesh. God, in taking the initiative, reconciled the world. Man, in turn, being reconciled through His death is saved by the life of Jesus. (Romans 5:1, 10) The act of God through Christ is effective to all who will accept the divine pronouncement through Christ

rule .... 1. an established regulation or guide for conduct, procedure, usage etc. 4. government; reign

S

source .... 1. a point of origin. 2. the place of origin of a stream of water 3. one that supplies information

springs v .... 4.comes into existence: arise **n.** 5 an origin or source

strength .... 1. the quality, state or property of being strong: power 2a. the power to resist force, stress or wear b) the power to resist attack. 4. intensity 5. firmness

sufficient .... as much as is needed or desired: enough

superseded .... 1. to take the place of: supplant 2. to set aside: displace

Marcella A. Spence

T
⁵transgression . . . . to break (a law, command, etc.); sin (against)
⁴trimmed . . . . 1. to neaten by clipping or pruning 2. to remove excess from by cutting

U
unrighteousness . . . . not in the right standing with God(AMP)

V
vainglorious . . . . boasting, pretentious display (AMP)
⁴vigilance . . . . alert watchfulness
¹virtue . . . . moral excellence, power
⁵vital . . . . 2. essential to life [vital organs] 4a. essential; indispensable b) very important

W
⁵whet . . . . 2. to stimulate
⁴wither . . . . 1. to shrivel or wilt from or as if from moisture loss 3. to render speechless or powerless

THE END

ACKNOWLEDGEMENTS
PERMISSIONS
REFERENCES

My sincerest thanks to **AuthorHouse Publishing** and its staff. Thank you and God Bless you all for walking me though my first two publications and to these publications and publishers for their permissions that made it possible for me to bring to you this book through the leading of the Holy Spirit.

AMPLIFIED BIBLE
COPYRIGHT   1954, 1958, 1962, 1964, 1965, 1987
by The Lockman Foundation
900 S. Euclid St. La Habra, CA 90631
(714) 879-3055
The Lockman Foundation
PO Box 2279
La Habra, CA 90632-2279
http://www.lockman.org

Used by permission from
AID TO BIBLE UNDERSTANDING
COPYRIGHT   1969, 1971
by Watchtower Bible & Tract Society of Pennsylvania Publishers
Watchtower Bible & Tract Society of NY, Inc.
International Bible Students Association
Brooklyn, NY USA
Pages 16, 17, 18

Marcella A. Spence

Used by permission from
2010/2011 TOWNSEND PRESS
SUNDAY SCHOOL COMMENTARY
BASED ON THE INTERNATIONAL LESSONS SERIES
COPYRIGHT   2010
by Committee on the Uniform Series of the
National Council of Churches USA
Sunday School Publishing Board
330 Charlotte Avenue
Nashville, TN 37201-1188
e-mail: customercare@sspbnbc.com
Pages 15, 16, 22
Thank you Wellington Johnson

[1]**Used by permission from**
THE NEW COMBINED BIBLE
DICTIONARY AND CONCORDANCE
written by Charles F Pfeiffer
Baker Books, a division of Baker Publishing Group
COPYRIGHT   1996 by C.D. Stampley Enterprises, Inc.
www.bakerpublishinggroup.com
Thank you David Greendonner

Used by permission from
[4]**WEBSTER'S NEW BASIC DICTIONARY**
THIRD EDITION
Copyright © by
Houghton Mifflin Harcourt Publishing Company.
Adapted and reproduced by permission from the Webster's New Basic
Dictionary.
Thank you Margaret Anne Miles

ABOUT THE AUTHOR

Without the experience that I had I would not know what it is to be rooted deeply in God's Love or grounded securely on His Love. I would not have come to know the breadth, the length, the height and true depth of God's Love. Without the Love of God there is absolutely nothing that you can overcome. With His Love comes all the things that you need to make you better, stronger and more at peace. That peace that has no understanding.

There is no love like God's Love. It is intense, it has no restrictions, it is extreme and it is in great detail.